DayOne

HELP!

I CAN'T GET MOTIVATED

Adam Embry

Consulting Editor: Dr. Paul Tautges

© Day One Publications 2011

First printed 2011

ISBN 978-1-84625-248-8

All Scripture quotations, unless stated otherwise, are from the English Standard Version, Crossway, 2001.

Published by Day One Publications
Ryelands Road, Leominster, HR6 8NZ

TEL 01568 613 740 FAX 01568 611 473

email—sales@dayone.co.uk

UK web site—www.dayone.co.uk

USA web site—www.dayonebookstore.com

Designed by **documen**
Printed by Orchard Press (Cheltenham) Ltd

To my parents

CONTENTS

Preface   6

Introduction   9

1   The Problem: Ruled by the Curse   14

2   The Consequence: The Curse of Death   22

3   The Solution: The Great Reversals   32

4   The Transformation: Work to Please God
    and Love Others   38

    Conclusion   45

    Personal Application Projects   49

    Where Can I Get Further Help?   63

PREFACE

Congratulations! By picking up this booklet you've taken the first step to overcoming your denial that you're not motivated!

Seriously, even though most self-help books say overcoming denial is the first step to recovery, this is no self-help booklet. We struggle with laziness and need divine help, not self-help. For this reason, this is a gospel-centered booklet. We're already self-centered enough, and that's part of the reason we lack motivation in different areas of our lives.

There are several reasons I have written this booklet. The senior pastor with whom I serve, Brian Croft (author of *Help! He's Struggling with Pornography*), and I preached five sermons through the book of Proverbs in the summer of 2010. One of my sermons was on the lazy person. The encouraging reaction from church members affirmed that the topic of laziness is one that is neglected but necessary for God's people to consider. This booklet is an adaptation and expansion of that sermon. I'd like to thank Brian for reading the manuscript and offering pastoral and theological suggestions that improved this work. Also, thanks go to Scott Wells and David Dykes for their biblical critiques and insight.

Another reason I have written this booklet is that our world presents us with many motivation killers. We have so much work to do, but who can get work done when we update our Facebook status every hour, watch every Saturday ballgame, sleep in too often, or just sit around doing nothing? Personal ease seems to be our greatest ambition. All of us have seen talented people fail to live up to their potential because they are unmotivated. There were no incentives that could motivate them because they didn't understand and live out the gospel.

The last reason I have written this booklet is that I myself am lazy. That sounds counterintuitive, because unmotivated people typically don't write books. Well, through this study of laziness I've discovered numerous ways that I waste time, lack motivation, and defame the name of Christ. This booklet is as much an indictment of my sin as it is an opportunity for you to consider in what way your lack of motivation is sinful. It is also a reminder of how much you and I need the gospel. Only its power will change our lives.

Adam Embry
Assistant Pastor
Auburndale Baptist Church
Louisville, Kentucky, USA

Have you seen those motivational posters that are so popular in the corporate world? Each black-bordered poster has a picture, usually of an object that is inspirational—like an eagle, a runner, or mountain range—along with a motivational buzzword like "leadership," "teamwork," "commitment," or "success," and a catchy phrase describing the motivational word. Imagine the meeting in the conference room as your boss explains a way to recover last quarter's company losses. He points to the poster behind him, hoping to motivate his employees. "Success," he reads from the poster. "Some people dream of success ... while others wake up and work hard at it." He concludes, "Let's get to work, people!"

But have you seen the de-motivational posters? They're a spoof on the motivational posters. Their humor and purpose are captured on their website in the phrase "increasing success by lowering expectations."[1] These posters look the same as the motivational ones, so they're equally recognizable. They're not meant to motivate, but to make fun of our faults and lack of motivation. Will reading a poster on success really motivate employees to greatness? Not likely! Here are the sayings from a few of the funnier posters: "Losing: If at first you don't succeed, failure may be your style." "Worth: Just because you're necessary doesn't mean you're important." Then there is the "Mistakes" poster. "Mistakes," your boss reads from the demotivational poster as he points to you. "It could be that the purpose of your life is only to serve as a warning to others." Obviously, such a poster never hangs in a conference room, but it is possibly in the mind of your boss.

People search everywhere for motivation, even on posters. We struggle to find the will and energy not only to get things done, but also to get things done with excellence. Does it really take financial incentives from our bosses or verbal pats-on-the-back from our spouses to get us to do our jobs or clean the house? Aren't we OK if we just acknowledge and laugh at our faults and lack of motivation? If we are

1 Visit Despair, Inc., at: despair.com/viewall.html.

Christians, we're supposed to do all things for God's glory (1 Corinthians 10:31), but why do we often find ourselves not wanting to do anything at all?

Sadly, even few Christians think often about the sinfulness of laziness. That is probably because we're unmotivated when it comes to examining sin in our lives, and that takes effort. Regardless, laziness was noted as a specific sin throughout the history of the church. Throughout the Middle Ages it was classified as one of the seven deadly sins: lust, gluttony, greed, wrath, envy, pride, and slothfulness (laziness). Christians guard against the lust of the flesh, the greed of the eyes, and the pride of life (1 John 2:16), but when it comes to laziness we often don't take any precautions. What we fail to realize is that being lazy provides the opportunity for other sins such as lust, greed, and pride to grow and take over our hearts. As the saying goes, "Idle hands are the devil's playground."

This booklet will help you observe what Scripture says about laziness in order that you may defeat it. The book of Proverbs describes the lazy man, and it is not difficult to observe him. Observing his senseless behavior gives us instruction on foolishness and wisdom (Proverbs 24:30). The unmotivated man doesn't move around much because he is too lazy to get out of bed. We'll get to hear this man mumble his excuses as he rolls over to sleep some more. Now, the lazy individual might look and sound comical, but laziness, contrary to the message of those demotivational posters, is no laughing matter.

The problem with laziness is that we fail to live as the people God created us to be. The imagery used in Scripture to describe the lazy individual was meant to remind God's people that the sin of laziness is rooted in the fall, when Adam and Eve, the first man and woman, disobeyed God in the Garden of Eden. The consequences of laziness are disastrous, as laziness destroys our well-being and our relationships with others, and, most importantly, it costs us our lives. So what is the solution? Buying a motivational poster? Having better self-esteem? Channeling our inner energies? No; the solution is the gospel: that Jesus Christ came to die for our sins. He paid the punishment we deserved for our sin—sin such as our laziness. He rose from the grave in order to give us spiritual life, to reconcile us to God, and to give us his perfect righteousness as a gift (1 Peter 3:18; 2 Corinthians 5:21). As a result, we can now live to please God. So how does transformation come from the gospel? It comes by understanding that laziness can be defeated when we work to please God and serve others.

My hope is that this booklet will help you defeat laziness and live a productive, motivated, God-glorifying life because of the gospel.

The Problem:
Ruled by the Curse

Why are we not motivated? To answer this we need to ask why we don't want to work and be productive. Deciding to give ourselves to laziness instead of living industriously is a result of sin. The problem with our lack of motivation is that our hearts do not want to work to serve God in anything we do. So how did our hearts get this way? We must first understand why God created us, and the tragic account of how humanity rejected that purpose.

God's design in creation was for humanity to reflect his character and rule the earth on his behalf. Put in scriptural terms, God made us in his image. The context of Genesis 1 makes that clear. Since God is the Ruler of the world, part of bearing his image means ruling the world on his behalf. God took divine counsel with himself and pronounced in Genesis 1:26–28:

"Let us make man in our image, after our
likeness. And let them have dominion ...
over all the earth ..." So God created man
in his own image, in the image of God he
created him; male and female he created
them. And God blessed them. And God said
to them, "Be fruitful and multiply and fill
the earth and subdue it and have dominion
over the fish ... and over the birds ... and
over every living thing ..."

Humanity is given control and dominion over the
earth on behalf of God. Genesis 2:15 records the
specific way Adam was to do this:

The LORD God took the man and put him
in the garden of Eden to work it and keep it.

Work, then, is God's idea. God himself is a
worker; he rested only after he created the universe
(Genesis 2:3). But after Adam and Eve sinned against
God and disobeyed his command not to eat from a
specific tree in the Garden, God pronounced a curse
on the ground that Adam worked. God's words are
recorded in Genesis 3:17–19:

> And to Adam he said, "Because you have
> listened to the voice of your wife and have
> eaten of the tree of which I commanded you,
> 'You shall not eat of it,' cursed is the ground
> because of you; in pain you shall eat of it all
> the days of your life; thorns and thistles it
> shall bring forth for you; and you shall eat
> the plants of the field. By the sweat of your
> face you shall eat bread, till you return to the
> ground, for out of it you were taken; for you
> are dust, and to dust you shall return."

The good, productive work Adam did in the Garden would now be laborious and painful, as he was kicked out of the Garden to cultivate the land in exile (Genesis 3:24). Adam was still to rule the earth for God—that command was never taken away—but he would do so through hard labor.[2] Instead of having a lush garden to work, Adam would labor with sweat and exhaustion against thorns and thistles of the hard earth. And, in the end, the very ground he tilled would defeat him, as Adam, who was taken from the earth, would return to it in death. Sin turned God's good plan of work into hard labor that ends in death.

2 The command to subdue the earth and rule it was reiterated after the fall in Genesis 9:1–7.

Yet Scripture records that humanity fought bravely against the thorns. Genesis chapters 4 and 11 both mention the creation of cities and culture—civilization. We have uprooted many thorns today as we have developed technology and medicine, or channeled solar and wind power. However, though humanity battles to uproot the thorns and take dominion over the earth, we can never defeat death. We can conquer the curse for only a little while. And so, at the end of life, we march in cadence with the words repeated throughout Genesis 5: "And he died … and he died … and he died."

Scripture records that the desire to conquer the curse proved unsustainable. If all that awaits us after a life of hard work is death, why should we work hard? This is why the author of Ecclesiastes asks honest questions we've all thought:

> What does man gain by all the toil
>   at which he toils under the sun?
>
> (1:3)

> What has a man from all the toil and
>   striving of heart with which he toils
>   beneath the sun?
>
> (2:22)

Many people today disobey God's command to subdue and have dominion over the earth by not working diligently and productively in a fallen world. We call such people "sluggards," "sloths," "slackers," "couch potatoes," "lazybones," or "loafers." Solomon, the great king of Israel, saw such a lazy individual and left us with this description:

> I passed by the field of a sluggard,
>   by the vineyard of a man lacking sense,
> and behold, it was all overgrown with thorns;
>   the ground was covered with nettles,
>   and its stone wall was broken down.
> Then I saw and considered it;
>   I looked and received instruction.
> A little sleep, a little slumber,
>   a little folding of the hands to rest,
> and poverty will come upon you like a
>   robber,
>   and want like an armed man.
>   (Proverbs 24:30–34)

One striking fact about these verses is that the lazy individual owns property. We're not told where he received it from. Perhaps he bought it, or perhaps it was passed down to him through the family. But, due to his laziness, the thorns overtook his land. A similar depiction of the lazy individual is in Proverbs 15:19:

> The way of a sluggard is like a hedge of thorns,
>   but the path of the upright is a level highway.

Charles Spurgeon, the famous British minister, preached a sermon on Proverbs 24:30–32 that highlighted the connection between Adam's duty in the Garden and the lazy man's sin:

> When God put Adam in the Garden of Eden
> it was not that he should walk through
> the glades and watch the spontaneous
> luxuriance of the unfallen earth, but that he
> might dress it and keep it, and he had the
> same end in view when he allotted each Jew
> his piece of land; he meant that the holy soil
> should reach the utmost point of fertility
> through the labor of those who owned it.
> Thus the possession of a field and a vineyard
> involved responsibilities upon the sluggard
> which he never fulfilled, and therefore he was
> void of understanding.[3]

3 C. H. Spurgeon, "The Sluggard's Farm," in *Farm Sermons* (London: [n.p.], 1882), 16.

In a farming society like Israel's, thorns were a part of life and in the Bible were always used negatively as a reminder of the curse in Genesis 3 that affects us and the earth.[4] The thorn imagery was so powerful that the Old Testament prophets used it in connection with Israel's exile, when Assyria and Babylon conquered them because of their sin. Thus in Isaiah's prophecy we read that Israel, God's vineyard, would be overgrown with "briers and thorns" (Isaiah 5:5–6) and "all the land will be briers and thorns" (Isaiah 7:23–25). Here, perhaps, is an echo of the condition that befell Adam when he and Eve were exiled from the Garden.[5]

The thorn imagery continues in the New Testament. Paul prayed for the removal of either a troubling situation or a sickness, something he described as a "thorn … in the flesh" (2 Corinthians 12:7). Jesus, the sinless descendant of Eve who crushed the head of Satan on the cross (Genesis 3:15), bore the curse we deserved as he died on that cross wearing a crown of thorns (John 19:2). Those who give no evidence of saving faith, the author of Hebrews argues, produce

---

4 "Thorns," in Leland Ryken, James C. Wilhoit, and Tremper Longman III (eds.), *Dictionary of Biblical Imagery* (Downers Grove, IL: IVP, 1998), 865.
5 Ibid.

thorns and thistles instead of a fruitful life that accompanies salvation (Hebrews 6:4–12).

So, in the Old Testament, and later in the New, thorn imagery represents the effects of the curse and sin, and this is the significance of the imagery in Proverbs 24:30–34 and 15:19 for the lazy individual. The thorns, representative of the curse, have conquered the lazy individual's land. Our laziness is rooted in the curse and sin.

Thus the Bible says that laziness is a decision to let sin and the curse rule. It is a failure to be a ruler in God's world. This is very important to recognize because the sin of laziness strikes at the heart of why God created humanity: to serve and obey him on earth. So why are we lazy? Because sin dominates us.

The problem of laziness is rooted in the problem that we are sinners, and as sinners we make excuses for our sin and bring devastating consequences upon ourselves. So, before we look at the solution, what excuses do we make for being lazy, and what are these devastating consequences that laziness brings?

The Consequence:
The Curse of Death

To best understand the consequences of not being motivated, we first need to hear the two excuses given by the lazy individual in the book of Proverbs. These two excuses give way to five serious consequences which impact our relationship with others and our well-being, and which ultimately lead to death.

Two Excuses

In Proverbs, the lazy man makes two main excuses. In fact, since he never works, he has plenty of time to conjure up excuses and talk about them. Charles Spurgeon said, "The slothful man is represented as having something to say, and I think that there are no people that have so much to say as those that have little to do. While nothing is done, much is talked about."[6]

The lazy man's first excuse is that he always needs to rest. In Proverbs 6:6–11 we hear how the lazy individual always needs a little nap:

> Go to the ant, O sluggard;
>   consider her ways, and be wise.
> Without having any chief,
>   officer, or ruler,
> she prepares her bread in summer
>   and gathers her food in harvest.
> How long will you lie there, O sluggard?
>   When will you arise from your sleep?
> A little sleep, a little slumber,
>   a little folding of the hands to rest,
> and poverty will come upon you like a
>   robber,
>   and want like an armed man.

The lazy person won't work because he or she "needs" just a little more sleep, slumber and rest.[7]

---

6 C. H. Spurgeon, "One Lion, Two Lions, No Lion at All," in *The Metropolitan Tabernacle Pulpit*, vol. 28 (London: [n.p.], 1882), 398.

7 The New American Standard Version supplies quotation marks around the phrase "A little sleep, a little slumber, a little folding of the hands to rest," and so attributes the words to the sluggard him- or herself.

This person's excuse for needing rest is really procrastination. You could imagine the individual saying today, "I'll just hit the snooze button on my alarm clock a few more times." Several more minutes' sleep then turn into hours, which turn into a wasted day.

In contrast to the lazy individual is the ant. Some Palestinian ants were known for storing up grain for the winter.[8] Rather than conquering creation by working for God, we are lazy and must learn from one of the smallest creatures, the ant, who instinctively works hard without being told to do so. The unmotivated person's sin leads to a reversal of his or her role as God's image bearer (Psalm 8:6–8).

The lazy man's second excuse is that it's just too risky heading off to work:

> The sluggard says, "There is a lion in the
>   road!
>   There is a lion in the streets!"
> As a door turns on its hinges,
>   so does a sluggard on his bed.
> The sluggard buries his hand in the dish;

---

8 Duane A. Garrett, *Proverbs, Ecclesiastes, Song of Songs* (Nashville: Broadman, 1993), 96.

> *it wears him out to bring it back to his*
> *mouth.*
> *The sluggard is wiser in his own eyes*
> *than seven men who can answer sensibly.*
> (Proverbs 26:13–16; compare 22:13)

The unmotivated person thinks that the remote danger of a lion roaming the streets is a reason to avoid work. Now, lions typically didn't roam the streets of Israel looking for an unmotivated person to devour. Here's the logic in today's world: "I can't drive to work! People die in car accidents!" Or, "I can't go outside to work! I might get struck by lightning!" Work is too wearisome to engage in and so he or she makes more excuses. In Proverbs, in his laziness the sluggard invented an imaginary lion, and this remote possibility of danger prohibited him from working. And this was sound, wise logic in his mind! There's no way you can talk the lazy person out of getting out of bed and going to work, because he or she has rationalized his or her pathetic excuses.

Five Consequences

The lazy person's two excuses lead to five serious consequences.

VIOLENT POVERTY

> ... And poverty will come upon you like a
>   robber,
>   and want like an armed man.
>   (Proverbs 6:11)

Financial and material loss won't take place over time; they'll take place suddenly, like a robber violently breaking into your house unannounced and holding you at gunpoint. In a split second the sluggard will lose everything because of his or her laziness.

LOSS OF FRIENDSHIP

> Like vinegar to the teeth and smoke to the
>   eyes,
>   so is the sluggard to those who send him.
>   (Proverbs 10:26)

Unmotivated people are annoying and unreliable for others. The doubly negative description of vinegar and smoke makes an emphatic point: the lazy person is a sour and irritating individual, someone who is completely annoying. Rather than being trusted and reliable, he or she is no help at all to anyone.

UNFINISHED TASKS

> Whoever is slothful will not roast his game,
>   but the diligent man will get precious
>   wealth.
>
>   (Proverbs 12:27; compare 19:24)

Remember how the lazy field-owner in Proverbs 24 owned property but didn't cultivate the land? Now we see that the lazy person never even cooks the animal he or she killed for dinner.

This person shot the animal, and this certainly tells us that he or she has the ability to work. But the lazy man or woman lacks the ambition to complete the task by skinning and cooking the animal to feed him- or herself, or worse, his or her family. What good is an uncooked carcass? It's like going to the grocery store, buying food, driving home, yet leaving the food in the car only to spoil. This person's laziness leads to unfinished tasks, even important ones like providing food.

UNFULFILLED DESIRES

> The soul of the sluggard craves and gets
>   nothing,
>   while the soul of the diligent is richly
>   supplied.
>
> (Proverbs 13:4)

Connected to the previous consequence is this: that unmotivated people never fulfill their desires. This verse uses the metaphor of eating to convey how the wise are filled and the lazy go hungry.

Likewise, in Proverbs 21:26, lazy people crave and crave, whereas the righteous are so filled with goodness that they can give freely to others:

> All day long he [the sluggard] craves and
>   craves,
>   but the righteous gives and does not hold
>   back.

Lazy individuals never fulfill their desires.

DEATH

> The desire of the sluggard kills him,
>> for his hands refuse to labor.
>
> (Proverbs 21:25)

The lazy person's laziness brings death. Lazy people want something—food, accomplishments, to live life to its fullest—but they won't put their hands to work, and so they die. A similar consequence is described in Proverbs 15:19–24, which again contrasts how the lazy man and the wise man walk down separate paths:

> The way of a sluggard is like a hedge of thorns,
>> but the path of the upright is a level highway.
>
> A wise son makes a glad father,
>> but a foolish man despises his mother.
>
> Folly is a joy to him who lacks sense,
>> but a man of understanding walks straight ahead.
>
> Without counsel plans fail,
>> but with many advisers they succeed.
>
> To make an apt answer is a joy to a man,
>> and a word in season, how good it is!

> The path of life leads upward for the
>   prudent,
>   that he may turn away from Sheol beneath.

The wise person walks down a path that leads to life, whereas the lazy person walks down to Sheol, which is an Old Testament term for the grave. There's no life in life itself for the lazy person, and so there's nothing that awaits but death. This person's refusal to be productive, dependable, cooperative, wise, and obedient to God ensures that his or her laziness results in what that person deserves: death.

These five consequences can be viewed from a different angle, as laziness negatively impacts our relationships with others (annoying/unhelpful), our well-being (poverty, unfinished tasks, unfulfilled desires), and our eternal destiny (death). The lazy individual's excuses epitomize an obsessive, selfish care for him- or herself, a disregard for others, and disobedience toward God. "Idleness," Spurgeon preached, "is selfishness, and this is not consistent with the love of neighbor, nor with any high degree of virtue."[9] Laziness, then, is a sin that dominates all of life and reflects disobedience to God's law. It's a curse we bring upon ourselves and our relationships that will ultimately kill us.

Slothfulness, like all other sins, is deceptive. We never think its consequences are catastrophic. It offers us ease and comfort, but it fails to deliver. Augustine noted this when he said, "Sloth poses as the love of peace: yet what certain peace is there besides the Lord?"[10] The solution to fighting laziness is the good news of salvation the Lord brings.

9   C. H. Spurgeon, "The Hedge of Thorns and the Plain Way," in *The Metropolitan Tabernacle Pulpit*, vol. 33 (London: [n.p.], 1887), 99.

10 Augustine, *Confessions* (New York: Penguin, 1961), 50.

The Solution: The Great Reversals

One of my favorite Christmas carols is "Joy to the World" by Isaac Watts. The third verse speaks of Jesus reversing the curse of sin:

No more let sins and sorrows grow,
Nor thorns infest the ground;
He comes to make his blessings flow
Far as the curse is found,
Far as the curse is found,
Far as, far as the curse is found.

This hymn echoes the New Testament's teaching that the curse of sin does not have the final say in our lives. Jesus's death on the cross and his resurrection from the dead reversed the curse of sin mentioned in Genesis 3:19: "to dust you shall return."

The Reversal of the Curse

The curse is reversed as the story of redemption in Scripture moves from the fall in the Garden to the death and resurrection of Jesus. The Old Testament clearly states that all who have sinned against God and his law deserve death. Deuteronomy 27:26 states,

> Cursed be anyone who does not confirm the words of this law by doing them.

Paul wrote in Romans 3:23 that everyone has sinned and failed to live up to God's glory. Yet Paul also wrote in Galatians 3:13 that Jesus bore the penalty of the curse for us:

> Christ redeemed us from the curse of the law by becoming a curse for us.

The reversal of the curse occurs because Jesus faithfully worked hard for and always obeyed his Father, even by dying on the cross (John 4:34). In contrast to the lazy fool who never finishes his or her tasks, Jesus triumphantly cried out at the cross, "It is finished" (John 19:30).

Now he reigns as supreme King over his people's hearts. This is why an angel showed the apostle John what awaits Christians in the new earth, when all his people will serve him:

> *No longer will there be anything accursed,*
> *but the throne of God and of the Lamb will*
> *be in it, and his servants will worship him.*
> (Revelation 22:3)

The biblical witness is undeniable. We deserved death because of our sin, sin such as laziness—but Jesus died in our place, reversed the curse, and made us God's servants. Because of Jesus, we can defeat laziness and its consequences.

The possibility of living a life in which we overcome the curse of sin is only available for those who have repented (turned away) from their sins and trusted in Jesus for their salvation. Consequently, believers in Jesus are no longer slaves to sin but slaves to righteousness (Romans 6:15-19). Believers serve a new Master, Jesus Christ, as Lord. When he saves us, he changes us, giving us hearts that want to serve him and others (Jeremiah 31:33). If you now recognize that you are a sinner but have never repented of your sin, I urge you to turn to Jesus today. He took the punishment of the curse that you deserved and now offers salvation.

The Reversal of Foolishness

The opening verses of Proverbs broadly describe two types of people: the wise person and the fool. The wise person will fear God and so learn from the observations given in Proverbs. The fool will show, by his or her rejection of Scripture's wisdom and instruction, that he or she does not fear God. As Proverbs 1:7 states,

> The fear of the LORD is the beginning of
>   knowledge;
>   fools despise wisdom and instruction.

Throughout Proverbs different characters are described as fools: the adulterer (6:32), deceiver (10:10), liar (10:18), arrogant (12:15), and angry (14:29). The sluggard lacks wisdom (6:6) and sense (24:30), and is therefore considered a fool. But does our lack of motivation really make us fools?

It has been said that Mark Twain once jokingly remarked, "Let us be thankful for fools, for without fools, the rest of us would never succeed." We often have the attitude the American novelist describes when we compare our lives with those of others and arrogantly think to ourselves, "At least I'm not as unmotivated or lazy as that person." The problem with this type of attitude is that it betrays Scripture's claim that laziness is foolishness. Though we might not think we're as foolish as other people (and thus feel thankful, like Twain), any lack of motivation to do something for God's glory is considered foolishness.

But there is good news for us all. Not only does Jesus reverse the curse of sin for believers, he also reverses our status as fools. Unlike the fools described in the book of Proverbs, Jesus is faithful, pure, truthful, humble, and gentle, and he does everything for God's glory. Everything he does is wise.

The apostle Paul explains in 1 Corinthians 1:30–31 that those who have repented of their sins and trusted in Jesus are now "in" Christ Jesus and receive his wisdom:

> And because of him you are in Christ
> Jesus, who became to us wisdom from
> God, righteousness and sanctification and
> redemption, so that, as it is written, "Let the
> one who boasts, boast in the Lord."

To be "in" Jesus means that we no longer live in the realm of sin and Satan, but instead our lives are now associated and connected to Jesus's life. As a result, we receive his wisdom.

Jesus, then, is our wisdom, just as he is our righteousness, holiness, and redemption. Just as we stand perfectly righteous before God because of Jesus (Romans 5:17), so now we receive Christ's wisdom. Were we fools because of our laziness? Yes. Do we have to live life as lazy fools? No. Can we be proud that we are no longer lazy fools? No. Can we boast that Jesus is the wisdom we did not have? Absolutely! Having Jesus as our wisdom means he will empower us to live wisely for him. So let us be thankful for Jesus, for without him we would all still be fools.

The gospel of salvation in Jesus reverses the curse of sin. The sorrow and sin that our laziness brings is defeated and reversed. No more will thorns infest the grounds of believers' hearts. We are also no longer fools, because Jesus Christ is ours. Because of the power of the gospel we are transformed and motivated to love God and our neighbors by working to please Jesus.

The Transformation:
Work to Please God and Love Others

How do we defeat laziness? The gospel presents two significant implications for how we understand work. Because of the cross we are now able to work hard with the right motives, and so honor God, bless our neighbors, and consequently fulfill the greatest commands: to love God and our neighbors (Mark 12:29–31).

Work to Please God

The first implication is that God is pleased when we willingly work for him because we love him. Passages such as Genesis 1:26–28 and 2:15 establish the idea that God made us to work. Work, then, is not a consequence or by-product of sin; it is a way to love God. Paul explains this in Ephesians 6:5–8:

> *Slaves, obey your earthly masters with fear*
> *and trembling, with a sincere heart, as you*
> *would Christ, not by the way of eye-service,*
> *as people-pleasers, but as servants of Christ,*
> *doing the will of God from the heart,*
> *rendering service with a good will as to the*
> *Lord and not to man, knowing that whatever*
> *good anyone does, this he will receive back*
> *from the Lord, whether he is a slave or free.*

Paul's concern is how believers can display the gospel in their occupations, even as slaves (slavery was common throughout the Roman Empire). The only way he can tell a slave to remain working under his master is if work itself is designed by God. As work is designed by God, he tells the slave to work for his master as if he were working for Christ, or as Christ's slave, "doing the will of God from the heart" (Ephesians 6:6). Someone who works for Christ demonstrates that he or she has been changed by the gospel, and also conveys that gospel to others through his or her actions.

Because we work primarily to please Christ regardless of our occupations, all jobs (barring those that are sinful) are dignified. Many people don't like or enjoy their careers. Perhaps you think that your job is not important because it is not prestigious. Your livelihood is not something you desire to do every day. (Demotivational poster: "Get to work: You aren't being paid to believe in the power of your dreams.") Or perhaps you have a significant job and it's more demanding than you expected. Rather than maintain a high level of performance, you've slacked off, thinking you deserve a break. These are not the attitudes Scripture says we should have. Throughout the Bible we find many godly individuals in common occupations, the "blue-collar jobs": chariot-drivers, farmers, carpenters, garment-makers, merchants, homemakers, and shepherds. We also see godly people holding significant occupations throughout Israel or the Roman Empire. Some of God's people were even despised government workers: the tax collectors. In summary, "The Bible presents no hierarchy of occupation," that is, no one is more or less holy because of the job he or she does.[11]

Understanding the dignity of work is one of the main results from the Protestant Reformation of the sixteenth century. Roman Catholic teaching divided the world into sacred and secular spheres: church jobs were sacred and special; everyone else's job was

---

11 "Work," in *Dictionary of Biblical Imagery*, 967.

secular or common. Martin Luther countered this mindset by stating,

> *What seem to be secular works [ordinary occupations in the world] are actually the praise of God and represent an obedience which is well pleasing to him ... Housework has no obvious appearance of holiness, yet these very household chores are more to be valued than all the works of monks or nuns ... The whole world could be filled with the service of God—not just the churches, but the home, the kitchen, the cellar, the workshop and the fields.*[12]

The English Reformer William Tyndale echoed Luther's teaching when he said, "The washing of dishes and preaching the word of God" represent different human activities but are both no different in pleasing God.[13] So, regardless of your occupation, if you work to please Christ, you fulfill God's plan in creating us to work. This is the attitude that displays that we have been changed by the gospel.

12 Cited by Alister McGrath, *Reformation Thought: An Introduction* (3rd edn.; Malden, MA: Blackwell, 1999), 265–266.
13 Ibid. 265.

Work to Show Love for Others

The second implication is that working hard shows we love others. Paul taught this to the church in Thessalonica. Some of the members of that church who could work refused to do so. Instead, they probably lived off the incomes and generosity of the church's wealthier members (Acts 17:4). Paul stated in 1 Thessalonians 4:9–12,

> Now concerning brotherly love you have
> no need for anyone to write to you, for you
> yourselves have been taught by God to love
> one another, for that indeed is what you
> are doing to all the brothers throughout
> Macedonia. But we urge you, brothers, to
> do this more and more, and to aspire to live
> quietly, and to mind your own affairs, and
> to work with your hands, as we instructed
> you, so that you may walk properly before
> outsiders and be dependent on no one.

These verses teach that there is a connection between loving others and working hard. Paul told the church to "excel more" at loving others by working hard. Love for fellow believers was a central

Christian virtue taught by Jesus (John 13:34). Refusing to work yet demanding financial support from the church was not a way to love others.[14] Paul states that independence, minding your own business, and earning your own income are ways to love fellow Christians because you aren't placing a burden on them to care for you unnecessarily.

Some of the Thessalonians, however, did not obey Paul's instruction. When he wrote to them again, he reiterated his point:

> Now we command you, brothers, in the
> name of our Lord Jesus Christ, that you
> keep away from any brother who is walking
> in idleness and not in accord with the
> tradition that you received from us. For you
> yourselves know how you ought to imitate
> us, because we were not idle when we were
> with you, nor did we eat anyone's bread
> without paying for it, but with toil and labor
> we worked night and day, that we might
> not be a burden to any of you. It was not
> because we do not have that right, but to

14 Paul's words in 1 Thessalonians 4 would obviously not apply to those who have physical or mental limitations, who are unable to work, or have lost their jobs.

> give you in ourselves an example to imitate.
> For even when we were with you, we would
> give you this command: If anyone is not
> willing to work, let him not eat. For we hear
> that some among you walk in idleness, not
> busy at work, but busybodies. Now such
> persons we command and encourage in the
> Lord Jesus Christ to do their work quietly
> and to earn their own living.
>
> (2 Thessalonians 3:6-12)

Paul's life and ministry presented to the undisciplined members of the Thessalonian congregation an example of hard work. Not only that, but Paul grounded his command and exhortation in the authority of Jesus. Refusing to work hard, therefore, takes advantage of others and is direct disobedience to Jesus. But our hope is that, just as the gospel transformed Paul's life, so it will transform ours. By God's grace, we can have hearts that are motivated to overcome laziness. Confessing our sin to God is the best place to start. Ask him to change your heart so that you can work for his glory and for the benefit of others. As you work, rely on Christ for grace, knowing that because of him you can be motivated to work for the right reasons.

CONCLUSION

The decision to let laziness rule our lives can be reversed by the power of the gospel of Jesus Christ. I have seen this take place not only in my life but also in the lives of others. Because of the gospel, the following people now defeat laziness by loving God and serving others.

Nick[15] is a high-energy, fun-loving graduate student who failed to live up to his potential. He frequently missed deadlines for school, and, as a result, had less time to spend with the church. After different conversations with his pastors, he eventually confessed his sin of laziness. Another church member met with him for weekly accountability. Nick got a day-planner and started getting assignments done early. Most importantly, he made a plan for daily Bible reading and prayer. Now he's got more time to

15 All names have been changed.

visit sick church members in the hospital, a ministry he's taken upon himself. When he understood that his time was really not his own but God's, he was motivated to put aside his laziness and be motivated for the right reason: because Jesus defeated his sin and changed his life. This allowed him to spend more time with church members and serve them.

Kevin is a businessman who was motivated for all the wrong reasons: big home, more money, and greater recognition. Unfortunately, these motivations were unable to make good on their promises. Debt strained his marriage, and church life was almost nonexistent. As a result, laziness set in as a remedy for all of life's worries and led him to return to his pre-conversion sins. He lost his will to get anything done. Kevin turned the corner when the Lord convicted him that he had a sinful misunderstanding of why he should work. He finally understood that his motivations were self-serving and were destroying his marriage and financial stability, potentially leading to church discipline. The pastor spent time counseling Kevin from Scripture, helping him to understand his patterns of sin and how Christ defeated them. Today, he is more motivated to work hard than he was before, but now for the right reasons. He wants the Lord to use him to display how the gospel has changed him. Only the Lord can bring about this type of change in someone's life.

With only one child to care for, Betty found that she had too much time on her hands at home. She became very lazy. The laundry got put off until another day, dishes piled up, and the floors were cluttered; but there was plenty of time to watch TV, read books, and surf the Internet. Challenged by other women in the church, she took time to meditate on the productive and godly woman described in Proverbs 31. Betty realized that her laziness was sinful; the Proverbs 31 woman worked hard because she feared the Lord (v. 30). Betty's laziness didn't display love to others but self-love. She made a weekly schedule for household chores that freed her up to minister to other moms in the church. Home soon became a place of peace for her hard-working husband, who noticed the godly change in his wife.

Each of these examples is meant to encourage you that the Lord can defeat laziness in your life. The curse and dominion of sin no longer rule over God's people, and so you too can live as the motivated image-bearer God made you to be. It is God's desire to see his children working hard to serve him and love others, and so he delivers them by giving them hearts that respond to his grace, defeat laziness, and find motivation to serve him and others. These three believers' lives demonstrate that the death and resurrection of Jesus did indeed reverse the curse of sin. The gospel is the only power that can truly motivate us to love God and others.

Personal Application Projects

There are three practical steps all of us can take to fight laziness. However, please understand that these steps are the fruit of a life that has been changed by Jesus. They must not replace the gospel. Anything we do practically in order to be motivated only occurs because of who we *are* now as Christians.

1. Make a Schedule

Make a schedule and keep to it. I'm one of those people who like to make lists merely so I can check off items when I complete them. You might not be as obsessive as me, but having a day-planner and recording your activities and responsibilities is a helpful tool for tracking what work needs to get done in your life. I have a weekly schedule, monthly schedule, and yearly schedule. Recorded are items that need to be completed every week, month, and year. For long-range items I plan an early due date so I don't have to wait until the last minute to accomplish a task. Some people work better under pressure, but the idea is to fight laziness by knowing your schedule. Consider how you can best start taking responsibility for your activities. If you're married, consider planning all events and jobs on a joint calendar. Once you've planned, pray over your schedule, knowing that the Lord will direct your steps (Proverbs 3:5–6).

2. Laziness vs Leisure Time

A paradigm shift needs to take place in our thinking about what we do with our time off from work. I'm not saying that you need to get a second job and never relax, but it can be helpful to make a distinction between laziness and leisure. Laziness tends to be self-centered, whereas our leisure time can focus on developing relationships and enjoying others. Having personal time after a hard day's work can help you reenergize to enjoy your family or friends. There's no harm in personal time, and there are plenty of leisure activities that we can do alone, like taking a walk, meditating on Scripture, or sitting on the front porch. For me, the danger is when I turn my personal time into an extended time away from family. For example, spending time alone reading a good book is good leisure time that helps me unwind so I can focus on spending time with the family. On the other hand, for me, spending time reading six science-fiction novels in one month was selfish laziness that took time away from enjoying my wife and children. Life is not all work and no play. When we're not at work, we should enjoy life, but not to the point that our leisure time turns into laziness that neglects others.

3. Examine Your Heart

Most importantly, we need to examine our hearts: we need to understand our motives and actions in light of God's Word. This means deliberately searching areas of our lives that show disobedience to Christ and guarding our hearts from those sins through God's grace. The motivation for examining our hearts comes from Proverbs 4:23, which encourages us to

> Keep your heart with all vigilance,
>   for from it flow the springs of life.

Examining our hearts for sin takes hard work. The

following list gives six categories with descriptions of our roles and duties as men and women and how laziness impacts them. Use the questions to help you think through how to watch your heart and defeat laziness.

HUSBANDS

Husbands have the wonderful privilege of providing for their families financially and spiritually (Ephesians 5:25–33; 6:4; 1 Peter 3:7). Laziness makes these already difficult tasks more difficult, because it takes responsibility off their shoulders and puts it onto their wives, making them carry a burden of leadership they should not have to carry. Being lazy affects men's relationships with their wives, who desire their attention and affection. Ensuring that your wife is your best friend and lover takes lifelong work.

Lazy men also negatively impact their local churches. All Christian men are potential leaders in the church, but lazy men who never socialize or engage in church activities ensure that the kingdom of God is not advanced as much as it could be through the church.

▶ *When am I most lazy? When does my wife say I'm lazy?*

▶ *In what areas of my family am I not leading? In what areas does my wife think I'm not leading?*

▶ *How do I use my time off from work? To entertain myself or invest in my family?*

▶ *Do I consistently not finish work but bring it home with me? What can I do to prevent this?*

▶ *Am I seeking to love my wife as Christ loved the church?*

▶ *How am I serving my church? Is there a ministry in which my pastor thinks I can or should serve? Is there a certain man in the church I can disciple?*

FATHERS

Fathers are entrusted with a special privilege of instructing their children.[16] Children are observant

---

16 Observe the numerous verses that emphasize a father's instruction to his son in Proverbs chapters 1–9 (1:8; 2:1; 3:1; 4:1; 4:10; 4:20; 5:1; 6:1; 6:20; 7:1; 7:24; 8:32). Also see Deuteronomy 6 and Ephesians 6:1–4.

and will notice when you decide to be lazy and focus on yourself instead of spending time with them. The temptation is to come home from a hard day's work and want the family to serve you instead of you serving them. The privilege of providing for the family does not end when the work day is over. Fathers must rely on God's grace to serve the family when off work. Lazy fathers abdicate their disciplinary role and so lose their parental authority. Passive discipline (e.g. letting your children throw tantrums instead of disciplining them) is lazy parenting. Infrequent discipline, or neglecting to discipline your children, places another burden on your wife and ensures you have no credibility when you finally decide to discipline. Disciplining your children is your duty, as it displays to them how our heavenly Father cares for and instructs us (Hebrews 12:4–11).

Questions for Fathers

▶ How much time do I spend instructing and playing with my children? In what areas of Christian truth do my children need instruction?

▶ Do I take the lead in disciplining my children, or do I do so only when my wife asks me?

▶ When am I least likely to discipline my children? Am I explaining the gospel to my children when I discipline them?

▶ Am I discussing family matters with my wife?

▶ Does my wife think I'm lazy with the family?

▶ Do I find myself wanting to entertain myself or spend leisure time with the family?

WIVES

The portrait of the industrious woman is the godly wife in Proverbs 31:10–31, a poem crafted with each verse beginning with a different letter of the Hebrew alphabet. This wife deals wisely and carefully with her family's goods and finances (vv. 16, 18). She works extremely hard caring for her family and others (vv. 20–21, 27). She stays up late and gets up early, working for her family (vv. 15, 18). The centerpiece of this poem is verse 23, a declaration that the husband is highly regarded by others in the community because of his wife's dedicated and productive life. As a result, the Proverbs 31 woman "is the kind of wife a man needs in order to be

successful in life."[17] A lazy wife, however, reflects
poorly on her husband, to whom she is to submit
(Ephesians 5:22–24). Godly wives also cultivate
spiritual beauty, which is pleasing to the Lord
(1 Peter 3:1–6).

Questions for Wives

▶ When am I most lazy? When does my husband
say I'm lazy?

▶ What areas of my family am I not serving?
In what areas does my husband think I'm
not serving?

▶ How do I use my time off from work?

▶ Do I consistently fail to finish housework or
office work?

▶ How am I cultivating spiritual beauty in my life?

▶ How can I serve my church? Is there a ministry
my pastor thinks I can serve? Is there another
lady I can disciple?

17 Garrett, *Proverbs, Ecclesiastes, Song of Songs*, 248.

MOTHERS

Lazy mothers, like lazy fathers, distance their children. Even though mothers have a special way of nurturing and loving their children, godly parenting still takes effort, time, teaching, and encouragement. Trust that both your husband and your children, by God's grace, will recognize your loving labors and praise you for your efforts (Proverbs 31:28). Laziness threatens all motherly duties and turns loving mothers into indifferent house-sitters. Children know whether or not you're interested in parenting and will misbehave accordingly.

Both stay-at-home mothers and working mothers must fight laziness. Stay-at-home mothers are able to implement daily schedules and routines that foster responsibility and stability for the children. The temptation is often to relax or break your schedule because you make it. Working mothers have less time at home with the family. The temptation is often not to serve the family when you come home from work. Both kinds of mothers must rely on God's grace to provide the motivation needed to serve the family in love.

Questions for Mothers

▶ *How much time do I spend instructing and playing with my children? In what areas of Christian truth do my children need instruction?*

▶ *When am I least likely to discipline my children? Am I explaining the gospel to my children after I discipline them?*

▶ *Am I discussing family matters with my husband?*

▶ *Does my husband think I'm lazy with the kids?*

▶ *Do I stick to my schedule or put things off to another day?*

▶ *What distracts me from my daily scheduled tasks?*

STUDENTS/SINGLES

Being a student (high-school or college) or being single is a unique time of life. Yet it is also one of the easiest times to breed discontentment and laziness (1 Corinthians 7). Not defeating laziness during these formative years can stunt the building of a strong foundation economically and socially. But this is not to say that you should work hard now to make money later; rather, the ability to defeat laziness now will make it easier to adjust later if you enter the role of a husband and father or wife and mother. I also know of several single adults who may never marry but have devoted their lives to successful careers, enabling them to invest financially into missionaries and seminary students. Their lives are a picture of the productive single individual in 1 Corinthians 7:32. Being productive as a single church member can have a lasting effect upon your church. A single man in my church invested time in visiting older members, teaching the children, and improving so much as a preacher that he is currently an assistant pastor. Rather than succumbing to laziness with the extra time he had, he used his time and talents wisely in the church as he worked full-time and finished his Master's degree.

Questions for Students/Singles

▶ How can I serve others in my church?

▶ Are there families I can spend time with to learn about marriage and parenting?

- Do other men or women in the church think I'm lazy?

- Am I giving 100% in my studies?

- Am I considering how what I learn now in school/college can apply to how I might one day lead and serve a family?

- How am I most tempted to waste time?

ELDERLY/RETIRED

The typical mindset is that retirement brings rest and relaxation. This might be true in regard to full-time employment, but it is not true concerning our service in our churches and families. Scripture shows how older men and women can mentor young believers. In Proverbs 4:3–4, the father who instructs his son was himself taught by his father. The cultivation of wisdom, then, is a family and generational endeavor. In Titus 2:3–5 Paul exhorts older women to disciple younger women. Paul also says that the church should provide for only those widows who have lived model Christian lives (1 Timothy 5:3–10).

If you think you may have squandered precious time in the past, it's never too late to invest your life into others in the church. Many younger adults would be more than willing to have you disciple them. Discipling can begin by inviting someone over for lunch or coffee and discussing the points the pastor made in the sermon, or talking about what it means to be a godly man or woman.

Questions for the Elderly/Retired

▶ Am I taking the initiative to spend time with younger men and women in the church?

▶ What young father or mother in the church can I disciple? Whom does my pastor think I should disciple?

▶ Am I using retirement money to serve the gospel or my comfort?

▶ Am I staying healthy and active?

▶ What do others in the church say about my involvement?

▶ Are my daily activities serving Christ and my family, or myself?

A WORD FOR THE PERFECTIONIST

Ironically, certain perfectionists can face the temptation to be lazy. There are times I put off work because I want the job to be perfect. This means I find motivation in the wrong place—pleasing man and not God. God wants us to be diligent workers who serve Christ wholeheartedly, but the desire for perfection can sinfully focus on pleasing others. Once again, laziness deceives us. If this description fits you, memorize and meditate on Ephesians 6:5–9 so that you can work hard and efficiently to please, not people, but Christ. Most importantly, know that the gospel is not for perfect people (which we are not) but for imperfect people (which all of us are).

Where Can I Get Further Help?

DeYoung, Kevin, *Just Do Something: A Liberating Approach to Finding God's Will* (Chicago: Moody, 2009)

Petty, James C., *Priorities: Mastering Time Management* (Phillipsburg, NJ: P & R, 2001)

Ryken, Leland, *Redeeming the Time: A Christian Approach to Work and Leisure* (Grand Rapids, MI: Baker, 1995)

Books in the *Help!* series include ...

Help! Someone I Love Has
Cancer (Howard, Deborah)
  ISBN 978-1-84625-217-4

Help! My Baby Has Died
(Weems, Reggie)
  ISBN 978-1-84625-215-0

Help! My Spouse Has Been
Unfaithful (Summers, Mike)
  ISBN 978-1-84625-220-4

Help! I Have Breast Cancer
(Frields, Brenda)
  ISBN 978-1-84625-216-7

Help! My Marriage Has
Grown Cold (Thomas, Rick)
  ISBN 978-1-84625-219-8

Help! He's Struggling with
Pornography (Croft, Brian)
  ISBN 978-1-84625-218-1

Help! My Toddler Rules the
House (Tautges, Paul & Karen)
  ISBN 978-1-84625-221-1

Help! Someone I Love Has
Been Abused (Newheiser, Jim)
  ISBN 978-1-84625-222-8

Help! I Can't Get Motivated
(Embry, Adam)
  ISBN 978-1-84625-248-8

Help! I'm a Single Mom
(Trahan, Carol)
  ISBN 978-1-84625-244-0

Help! I'm a Slave to Food
(McCoy, Shannon)
  ISBN 978-1-84625-242-6

Help! I'm Confused about
Dating (James, Joel)
  ISBN 978-1-84625-247-1

Help! I'm Drowning in Debt
(Temple, Dr. John)
  ISBN 978-1-84625-249-5

Help! My Teen Is Gay
(Marshall, Ben)
  ISBN 978-1-84625-243-3

Help! My Teen Is Rebellious
(Coats, Dave & Judi)
  ISBN 978-1-84625-245-7

Help! She's Struggling with
Pornography (Coyle, Rachel)
  ISBN 978-1-84625-246-4

(More titles in preparation)